2-14-03

Happy Valentine's Day
Sarah
your friend, Connie

Truly Mars and Venus

JOHN GRAY, Ph.D.

Truly
Mars & Venus

THE ILLUSTRATED ESSENTIAL
Men Are from Mars,
Women Are from Venus

Illustrations by Barbara Slate

HarperCollins*Publishers*

HarperCollins books may be purchased for educational, business, or sales promotional use. For information, please write: Special Markets Department, HarperCollins Publishers Inc., 10 East 53rd Street, New York, NY 10022.

FIRST EDITION

Designed by Barbara Slate and Adrian Leichter

Printed on acid-free paper

Library of Congress Cataloging-in-Publication Data is available upon request.

ISBN 0-06-008565-7

03 04 05 06 07 ❖/RRD 10 9 8 7 6 5 4 3 2 1

*This book is dedicated with deepest love
and affection to my wife, Bonnie Gray.
Her love, vulnerability, wisdom, and strength
have inspired me to be the best I can be
and to share what we have learned together.*

Acknowledgments

I thank my wife, Bonnie, for sharing the journey of developing this book with me.

I thank our three daughters, Shannon, Juliet, and Lauren, for their continuous love and support. Living with four Venusians has certainly expanded my ability to understand and honor the female point of view.

I thank Barbara Slate for her tremendous contribution of designing and drawing the illustrations.

I thank my editor, Meaghan Dowling, at HarperCollins, for her brilliant feedback and advice. I also thank my publicist, Leslie Cohen, and the incredible staff at HarperCollins.

I thank Linda Michaels, my international agent, for getting my books published in more than fifty languages. I thank Monique Mallory at Planned Television Arts for her hard work in organizing my busy media schedule.

I thank my staff—Rosie Lynch, Michael Najarian, Donna Doiron, and Jeff Owens—for their consistent support and hard work marketing my radio show, books, tapes, seminars, and speaking engagements.

I thank my parents, Virginia and David Gray, for their love and encouragement. Though they are no longer here, their love continues to surround and support me.

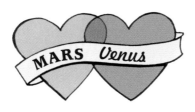

Introduction

Times have certainly changed, but on the inside men and women still have some very significant differences. When a man gets married he still hopes his wife will stay the same, while she still hopes that after their marriage he will change. Men continue to wonder what will make a woman happy, while women tend to overanalyze a man's behavior. When he is quiet and withdrawn, she wonders, "Does he love me, did I say something wrong, are we drifting apart, did I do something to bother him? . . ." In reality, he is probably just wondering what's on TV.

Never in history have men and women been so close. Not only are men wanting to spend more time on romance, women are working side by side with men in the office.

Although we are definitely becoming more similar, it doesn't mean we are the same or that we need to be the same. It is our differences that attract us to each other. Differences make our partners interesting and attractive. Yet it is also our differences that create problems. The biggest problem, however, is our tendency to expect our partners to think and feel the way we do. By reading *Truly Mars and Venus,* and remembering that men are from Mars and women are from Venus, this most important problem is easily solved.

Our gender differences are most easily understood and resolved by approaching them with a sense of humor. Men and women in my seminars often thank me for presenting this information in a playful and humorous manner. With smiles on their faces they are able to open up and really hear the message. Throughout *Truly Mars and Venus,* in this humorous way, men gain the insight to answer their age-old question, "What makes a woman happy?" On the other hand, a woman begins to understand the reasons behind what she considers to be a man's often bizarre behavior.

For example, she will understand, "Why does a man tend to ignore a woman after he has just spent quality time together?" or in other words, why he doesn't call. A man will understand certain basic ideas like, "Why does a woman talk to a man about problems when she is not looking for a solution?" or why sometimes she talks about problems that have no solution. So many mysteries, and so much fun to solve them.

On Mars, if you can't solve a problem, then the solution is to forget it and move on. On Venus, their philosophy is different: "If we can't solve it, then at least we talk about it." By understanding our different approaches to stress and problem solving, both men and women can learn to be more supportive than ever before.

It is not the case that we don't want to be supportive. No one wakes up in the morning thinking, "How can I annoy my partner today." (At least in the beginning.) When we fall in love, we all want to give our best. The hidden problem is that our best is not always what our partner is wanting and needing most. We automatically tend to give the support we would want and not what our partner really wants.

As a man, if I am not in a good mood, I will often want to be left alone and, in a friendly way, be ignored until my mood changes. The last thing I want is to be questioned about how I feel. A woman, however, will expect her partner to notice and ask her caring questions about her day. Without this information about our differences, if she was having a bad hair day, I would simply ignore her in a friendly manner, mistakenly concluding that I was being supportive. She would in turn wonder, "How could he be ignoring me at a time when I need him the most. Doesn't he care about me anymore?" By this simple misunderstanding, her mood would get worse instead of improve. By trying to be supportive, I would have unknowingly made things worse.

Throughout *Truly Mars and Venus* you will discover the many ways we often give what we want when that is not necessarily what our partner wants. Within a few days you will gain the insight required to make sure the love you feel in your heart is successfully communicated through your actions and reactions. In this short and easy-to-read book, you will get the essence of all my Mars Venus Books and discover the many secrets of life on Mars and Venus. While for some, it does not replace the need for a more in-depth study of our differences, it does immediately open our minds and hearts to a much more successful way of relating to one another.

This little book isn't just a practical manual for successful relationships, it is also a fun read. You, like the thousands of others who have attended my Mars Venus seminars, will laugh your way through the many examples of how we commonly misunderstand and unnecessarily frustrate each other. Not only does this simple message enrich happy relationships, but it has also saved thousands of marriages that were in serious trouble.

As a marriage counselor for the last thirty years, I have found that the most important insight I have gained is that all big problems first began as little problems that were not resolved. When little and easy-to-address problems are not solved, then inevitably they turn into big problems that seem to have no solution. By going back to address the little problems and by successfully addressing them, automatically the big and apparently unsolvable problems begin to disappear.

I truly believe that as men and women begin to understand and appreciate their innate differences, our dreams of lasting love can be realized. Divorce rates will go back down and couples will enjoy a lifetime of love. I believe it because I see it around me every day. I also trust that as men and women come together at home, this new harmony will be reflected in the world. Peace and a harmony between different nations finally becomes a possibility when we can first achieve this task at home.

The love you share today not only enriches you, your partner, and your children, but the world as well. I hope you enjoy reading this book and then share it with a friend. We have a lot to look forward to. May you continue to grow in love and light. Thank you for letting me make a difference in your life.

Truly Mars and Venus

CHAPTER 1

*When men and women are able
to respect their differences,
then love has a chance to grow.*

Men Are from Mars,

Imagine that men are from Mars and women are from Venus. One day long ago the Martians, looking through their telescopes, discovered the Venusians. Just glimpsing the Venusians awakened feelings they had never known. They fell in love and quickly invented space travel and flew to Venus.

The Venusians welcomed the Martians with open arms. They had intuitively known that this day would come. Their hearts opened wide to a love they had never felt before.

The love between the Venusians and Martians was magical. They delighted in being together, doing things together, and sharing together. Though from different worlds, they reveled in their differences. They spent months learning about each other, exploring and appreciating their different needs, preferences, and behavior patterns. For years they lived together in love and harmony.

Then they decided to fly to Earth. In the beginning everything was wonderful and beautiful. But the effects of Earth's atmosphere took hold, and one morning everyone woke up with a peculiar kind of amnesia—*selective amnesia!*

Women Are from Venus

Both the Martians and Venusians forgot that they were from different planets and were supposed to be different. In one morning everything they had learned about their differences was erased from their memory. And since that day men and women have been in conflict.

 ## Martians

1. Biggest mistake: Martians interrupt by offering solutions.

2. Men speak Martian.

3. Martians need to learn the importance of listening.

4. On Mars, big expressions of love make a big difference.

5. To feel better, men go into their caves.

6. On Mars, he assumes that if she is not asking for more then he must be giving enough.

7. Martians particularly enjoy being appreciated, accepted, and trusted.

Certainly within every Martian there is some Venusian.

DIFFERENCES

Venusians

1. Biggest mistake: Venusians offer unsolicited (helpful) advice.

2. Women speak Venusian.

3. Venusians need to learn how to stop trying to change a man.

4. On Venus, little expressions of love make a big difference.

5. To feel better, women discuss it.

6. On Venus, it's not romantic if she has to ask for expressions of love and affection.

7. Venusians particularly enjoy being respected, understood, and cherished.

Certainly within every Venusian there is some Martian.

LIFE ON MARS

*A man's sense of self is defined
through his ability to achieve results.*

Martians value power, competency, efficiency, and achievement. They are always doing things to prove themselves and develop their power and skills. Their sense of self is defined through their ability to achieve results. They experience fulfillment primarily through success and accomplishment.

They are more interested in "objects" and "things" rather than people and feelings. While women fantasize about romance, men fantasize about powerful cars, faster computers, and new, more powerful technology. Men are preoccupied with the "things" that can help them express power by creating results and achieving their goals.

A woman, however, may feel excluded, because when a man focuses on his work or on solving problems, she feels he doesn't care about her feelings.

LIFE ON VENUS

A woman's sense of self is defined through her feelings and the quality of her relationships.

Venusians value love, communication, beauty, and relationships. They spend a lot of time supporting, helping, and nurturing one another. Communication is of primary importance. Talking and relating to one another is a source of tremendous fulfillment.

On Venus, everyone studies psychology and has at least a master's degree in counseling. They are very involved in personal growth, spirituality, and everything that can nurture life, healing, and growth. Venus is covered with parks, organic gardens, shopping centers, and restaurants.

Venusians are very intuitive. They have developed this ability through centuries of anticipating the needs and feelings of others. A sign of great love is to offer help and assistance to another Venusian without being asked. A man, however, may feel offended, because when a woman offers advice, he doesn't feel she trusts his ability to do it himself.

When we remember

men are from Mars,

women are from Venus,

then everything can be explained.

Without the awareness that we are supposed to be different, men and women are at odds with each other. We usually become angry or frustrated because we have forgotten this important truth. We expect the opposite sex to be more like ourselves. We desire them to "want what we want" and "feel the way we feel."

By understanding the hidden differences of the opposite sex we can more successfully give and receive the love that is in our hearts. By validating and accepting our differences, creative solutions can be discovered whereby we can succeed in getting what we want. And, more important, we can learn how to best love and support the people we care about.

Love is magical, and it can last, if we remember our differences.

The most frequently expressed complaint women have about men is that men don't listen.

CHAPTER 2

The most frequently expressed complaint men have about women is that women are always trying to change them.

The Essential Mars Venus Test

When you take this test, be sure to go to a quiet place where you can answer the questions fairly and honestly. Both Martians and Venusians should take it; however, only **you** need to know how you scored.

(Martians usually hate tests
so don't expect him to share his answers.)

ARE YOU <u>REALLY</u> LISTENING TO HER?

Take this test to find out if you are a good listener. Score **one** point for each phrase (or similiar message) you say occasionally, **two** points for each phrase you say fairly often, and **three** points for habitual use.

1. "You shouldn't worry so much."

2. "But that is not what I said."

3. "It's not such a big deal."

4. "OK, I'm sorry. Now can we just forget it."

5. "Why don't you just do it?"

6. "But we do talk."

7. "You shouldn't feel hurt."

8. "So what are you trying to say?"

9. "But you shouldn't feel that way."

10. "How can you say that? Last week I spent the whole day with you. We had a great time."

11. "That's not what I meant."

12. "All right. I'll clean up the backyard. Does that make you happy?"

When a man loves a woman he mistakenly thinks he's helping her by becoming Mr. Fix-It and offering solutions to her problems. What she really wants is his empathy and understanding.

13. "I got it. This is what you should do.

14. "Look, there's nothing we can do about it."

15. "If you are going to complain, then don't do it."

16. "Why do you let people treat you that way?"

17. "If you're not happy, then we should just get a divorce."

18. "All right, then you can do it from now on."

19. "I'll handle it."

20. "Of course I care about you. That's ridiculous."

21. "Would you get to the point?"

22. "All we have to do is . . ."

23. "That's not at all what happened."

Martian Test Results

Are you REALLY listening to her?

Add up the points for your score.

0–10 points

Congratulations! You are a wonderful listener. You are supportive, trusting, and deserve a night out on the town from your Venusian.

10–21 points

Sometimes you don't listen, but for the most part, you are an attentive partner.

Over 21 points

You are not a good listener. For the next week, practice listening whenever a woman speaks. Practice biting your tongue whenever you get the urge to offer a solution or change how she is feeling. You will be surprised when you experience how much she appreciates you.

ARE YOU STILL TRYING TO IMPROVE HIM?

Take this test to find out your level of acceptance. Score **one** point for each phrase (or similiar message) you say occasionally, **two** points for each phrase you say fairly often, and **three** points for habitual use.

1. "How can you think of buying that?

2. "Those dishes are still wet. They'll dry with spots."

3. "Your hair is getting kind of long, isn't it?"

4. "There's a parking spot over there. Turn the car around."

5. "You want to spend time with your friends, what about me?"

6. "You shouldn't work so hard. Take a day off."

7. "Don't put that there. It will get lost."

8. "You should call a plumber. He'll know what to do."

9. "Why are we waiting for a table? Didn't you make reservations?"

10. "You should spend more time with the kids. They miss you."

11. "Your office is still a mess. How can you think in here? When are you going to clean it up?"

12. "You forgot to bring it home *again*."

13. "You're driving too fast. Slow down or you'll get a ticket."

When a woman loves a man she sets up the Home Improvement Committee and focuses on him. What he really wants is her trust and acceptance.

14. "Next time we should read the movie reviews."

15. "I didn't know where you were. You should have called."

16. "Somebody drank from the juice carton."

17. "Don't eat with your fingers. You're setting a bad example."

18. "Those potato chips are too greasy. They're not good for your heart."

19. "You are not leaving yourself enough time."

20. "I can't just drop everything and go to lunch with you."

21. "Your shirt doesn't match your pants."

22. "Bill called for the third time. When are you going to call him back?"

23. "Your toolbox is such a mess. I can't find anything. You should organize it."

Venusian Test Results

Are you still trying to improve him?

Add up the points for your score.

0–10 points

Congratulations! You have learned to accept your partner just the way he is. You deserve a special dinner from your Martian.

10–20 points

You still want to improve him, but for the most part, you are a supportive partner.

Over 21 points

Yes! You are *still* trying to improve him. For the next week, practice restraining from giving any unsolicited advice or criticism. The men in your life will not only appreciate it, but they will be more attentive and responsive to you.

*To feel better, Martians go to their caves
to solve problems alone.*

CHAPTER 3

*To feel better, Venusians get together
and openly talk about their problems.*

Men Go to Their Caves and Women Talk

One of the biggest differences between men and women is how they cope with stress. Men become increasingly focused and withdrawn while women become increasingly overwhelmed and emotionally involved. At these times, a man's needs for feeling good are different from a woman's. He feels better by solving problems while she feels better by talking about problems. Not understanding and accepting these differences creates unnecessary friction in our relationships.

WHY MEN GO INTO THEIR CAVES

1. He needs to think about a problem and find a practical solution.

2. He doesn't have an answer to a question. Men were never taught to say "Gee, I don't have an answer. I need to go into my cave and find one."

3. He has become upset or stressed. At such times he needs to be alone to cool off and find his control again. He doesn't want to do or say anything he might regret.

4. He needs some "space" or distance. When men are in love, at times they need to back up and regroup. Too much intimacy can create boredom on Mars; distance makes the heart grow fonder.

WHY WOMEN TALK

1. To convey or gather information.

2. To discover, explore, and develop what it is she wants to say.

3. To feel better and more centered when she is upset.

4. To create intimacy. By sharing her inner feelings, she feels more connected to others and to herself.

FIVE COMMON MISUNDERSTANDINGS

When a man is stuck in his cave, he is powerless to give his partner the quality attention she deserves. It is hard for her to be accepting of him at these times because she doesn't know how stressed he is. When he doesn't talk, she feels he is ignoring her. She mistakenly assumes he doesn't care because he isn't talking.

1. When a man is in the cave, he can record what she is saying with the 5 percent of his mind that is listening. He reasons he is listening to her. However, what she is asking for is his full, undivided attention.

2. He reasons that if his body is present, then she shouldn't say he is not there. However, she doesn't feel his full presence.

3. He reasons that because he is preoccupied with solving a problem that will in some way benefit her, she should know he cares. However, she needs to feel his direct caring through empathy and understanding.

4. He reasons that her feelings are invalid because his working benefits her. He doesn't realize that when he focuses on work and ignores her, she may take it personally.

5. In his cave, a man is unaware of how his indifferent attitude might feel to others. He reasons that she is being too critical and demanding because he is doing something that is essential for him to solve problems. However, what she needs is his empathy and time before he offers solutions.

Finding Relief Through Talking

When a woman is stressed she instinctively feels a need to talk about her feelings and all the possible problems that are associated with them. When she begins talking she does not prioritize the significance of any problem. If she is upset, then she is upset about it all, big and small. She is not immediately concerned with finding solutions to her problems but rather seeks relief by expressing herself and being understood. By randomly talking about her problems, she becomes less upset.

When women talk about problems, men usually resist. A man assumes she is talking with him about her problems because she is holding him responsible. The more problems, the more he feels blamed. He does not realize that she is talking to feel better. A man doesn't know that she will appreciate it if he just listens.

How the Martians and Venusians Found Peace

The Martians and Venusians lived together in peace because they were able to respect their differences. The Martians learned to respect that Venusians needed to talk to feel better. Even if the Martians didn't have much to say, they learned that by listening they could be very supportive. The Venusians learned to respect that Martians needed to withdraw to cope with stress. The cave was no longer a great mystery or cause for alarm.

SIX WAYS TO SUPPORT A MAN IN HIS CAVE

 1. Don't disapprove of his need to withdraw.

 2. Don't try to help him solve his problem by offering solutions.

 3. Don't try to nurture him by asking questions about his feelings.

 4. Don't sit next to the door of the cave and wait for him to come out.

 5. Don't worry about him or feel sorry for him.

 6. Do something that makes you happy.

call a friend

read a book

take a bath

tend the garden

write in a journal

listen to music

HE GOES INTO HIS CAVE

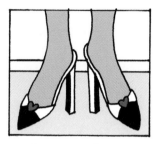

buy new shoes

pray/meditate

get a massage

see a therapist

watch TV

exercise

CHAPTER 4

*The enormous task of figuring out
what our partner needs is simplified
greatly through understanding the
twelve different kinds of love.*

The Twelve Primary Love Needs

Men and women are generally unaware that they have different emotional needs. As a result, they do not instinctively know how to support each other. Men typically give in relationships what men want, while women give what women want. Each mistakenly assumes that the other has the same needs and desires.

SHE NEEDS CARING

• • • • •

HE NEEDS TRUST

When a man shows interest in a woman's feelings and heartfelt concern for her well-being, she feels loved and cared for. When he makes her feel special in this caring way, he succeeds in fulfilling her first primary need. Naturally, she begins to trust him more, and becomes more open and receptive.

• • • • •

To trust a man is to believe that he is doing his best and that he wants the best for his partner. When a woman's reactions reveal a positive belief in her man's abilities and intentions, his first primary love need is fulfilled. Automatically he is more caring and attentive to her feelings and needs.

SHE NEEDS UNDERSTANDING

· · · · ·

HE NEEDS ACCEPTANCE

When a man listens without judgment but with empathy to a woman express her feelings, she feels heard and understood. The more a woman's need to be heard and understood is fulfilled, the easier it is for her to give her man the acceptance he needs.

· · · · ·

When a woman lovingly receives a man without trying to change him, he feels accepted. When a man feels accepted it is much easier for him to listen and give her the understanding she needs and deserves.

SHE NEEDS RESPECT

· · · · ·

HE NEEDS APPRECIATION

When a man responds to a woman in a way that acknowledges her rights, wishes, and needs, she feels respected. Concrete and physical expressions of respect, like flowers and remembering anniversaries, are essential to fulfill a woman's third primary love need. When she feels respected it is much easier for her to give her man the appreciation he deserves.

· · · · ·

When a woman acknowledges having received personal benefit and value from a man's efforts and behavior, he feels appreciated. When a man is appreciated he knows his effort is not wasted and is thus encouraged to give more. When a man is appreciated, he respects his partner more.

SHE NEEDS DEVOTION

• • • • •

HE NEEDS ADMIRATION

When a man gives priority to a woman's needs and proudly commits himself to supporting and fulfilling her, her fourth primary love need is fulfilled. A woman thrives when she feels adored. When a woman feels that she is number one in his life, then, quite easily, she admires him.

• • • • •

Just as a woman needs to feel a man's devotion, a man has a primary need to feel a woman's admiration. To admire a man is to regard him with wonder, delight, and pleased approval. When a man feels admired, he feels secure enough to devote himself to his woman and adore her.

SHE NEEDS VALIDATION

· · · · ·

HE NEEDS APPROVAL

When a man does not object to a woman's feelings but instead accepts their validity, she truly feels loved because her fifth primary need is fulfilled. (He can validate her point of view while having a different opinion.) When a man learns this validating attitude, he is assured of getting the approval he primarily needs.

· · · · ·

Deep inside, every man wants to be his woman's knight in shining armor. The signal that he has passed her tests is her approval. (Giving approval doesn't always mean agreeing with him.) An approving attitude recognizes the good reasons behind what he does. When he receives the approval he needs, it becomes easier for him to validate her feelings.

SHE NEEDS REASSURANCE

· · · · ·

HE NEEDS ENCOURAGEMENT

When a man repeatedly shows that he cares and is devoted to his partner, her primary need to be reassured is fulfilled. A reassuring attitude tells a woman that she is continually loved.

· · · · ·

To fulfill her sixth primary love need he must remember to reassure her again and again.

A man commonly makes the
mistake of thinking that once he has
met all of a woman's primary love
needs, and she feels happy and secure,
she should know from then on
that she is loved.

A man primarily needs to be encouraged by a woman. A woman's encouraging attitude gives hope and courage to a man by expressing confidence in his abilities and character. When a woman's attitude expresses trust, acceptance, appreciation, admiration, and approval, it encourages a man to be all that he can be. Feeling encouraged motivates him to give her the loving reassurance she needs.

CHAPTER 5

When a man loves a woman,
periodically he needs to pull away
before he can get closer.

Men Are Like Rubber Bands

Men are like rubber bands. When they pull away, they can stretch only so far before they come springing back. A rubber band is the perfect metaphor to understand the male intimacy cycle. This cycle involves getting close, pulling away, and then getting close again.

Men instinctively feel this urge to pull away. It is not a decision or choice. It just happens. It is neither his fault nor her fault. It is a natural cycle.

A man pulls away to fulfill his need for independence or autonomy. When he has fully stretched away, then instantly he will come springing back. When he has fully separated, then suddenly he will feel his need for love and intimacy again. Automatically, he will be more motivated to give his love and receive the love he needs. When a man springs back, he picks up the relationship at whatever degree of intimacy it was when he stretched away. He doesn't feel any need for a period of getting reacquainted again.

Certainly a man may pull away if he feels rejected, but he will also pull away even if she has done nothing wrong. He may love and trust her, and then suddenly he begins to pull away. Like a stretched rubber band, he will distance himself and then come back all on his own.

Women misinterpret a man's pulling away because generally a woman pulls away for different reasons. She pulls back when she doesn't trust him to understand her feelings, when she has been hurt and is afraid of being hurt again, or when he has done something wrong and disappointed her.

A man automatically alternates between
needing intimacy and autonomy.

Two Ways Venusians Obstruct

1. Chasing him when he pulls away.

Martians' Natural Intimacy Cycle

Chasing Behavior

- When he pulls away, she physically follows him. He may walk into another room and she follows.

- When he pulls away, she emotionally follows him. She worries about him. She wants to help him feel better. She feels sorry for him.

- She disapproves of his need to be alone.

- She looks longingly or hurt when he pulls away.

- She may try to pull him back by asking him guilt-inducing questions such as "How could you treat me this way?" or "What's wrong with you?" or "Don't you realize how much it hurts when you pull away?"

- She becomes overly accommodating. She tries to be perfect so he would never have any reason to pull away. She gives up her sense of self and tries to become what she thinks he wants.

2. Punishing him for pulling away.

When a man is punished for pulling away,
he may be afraid of ever doing it again.
This fear may prevent him from pulling away
in the future. His natural cycle is then broken.

Punishing Behavior

- When he begins to desire her again, she rejects him.

- When he returns, she is unhappy and blames him. She expresses her disapproval through words, tone of voice, and by looking at her partner in a wounded way.

- When he returns, she refuses to open up and share her feelings. She becomes cold and resents him for not opening up and talking.

- She stops trusting that he really cares and punishes him by not giving him a chance to listen and be the "good" guy.

WHAT EVERY WOMAN

If a man does not have the opportunity

to pull away, he never gets a chance to feel

his strong desire to be close. It is essential

for women to understand that if they

insist on continuous intimacy...

SHOULD KNOW ABOUT MEN

or "run after" their partner when

he pulls away, then he will almost always

be trying to escape and distance himself;

he will never get a chance to feel his

own passionate longing for love.

Tell me about your day.

THE WISE MARTIAN

Men generally don't realize how their suddenly pulling away and then later returning affects women. With this new insight about how women are affected by his intimacy cycle, a man can recognize the importance of sincerely listening when a woman speaks. He understands and respects her need to be reassured that he is interested in her and he does care. Whenever he is not needing to pull away, the wise man takes the time to initiate conversation.

Thanks for listening. It really helps.

THE WISE VENUSIAN

To initiate a conversation the wise woman learns not to demand that a man talk but asks that he truly listen to her. She trusts that he will gradually open up. She does not punish him or chase after him. She understands that sometimes her intimate feelings trigger his need to pull away while at other times (when he is on his way back) he is quite capable of hearing her intimate feelings.

CHAPTER 6

*In relationships, men pull back
and then get close, while women rise
and fall in their ability to love
themselves and others.*

Women Are Like Waves

When she feels loved, her self-esteem rises and falls in a wave motion. When she is feeling really good, she will reach a peak, but then suddenly her mood may change and her wave crashes down. This crash is temporary. After she reaches bottom, suddenly her mood will shift and she will again feel good about herself. Automatically, her wave begins to rise back up.

When a woman's wave rises she feels she has an abundance of love to give, but when it falls she feels her inner emptiness and needs to be filled up with love. This time of bottoming out is a time for emotional housecleaning.

If she has suppressed any negative feelings or denied herself in order to be more loving on the upswing of her wave, then on the downswing she begins to experience these negative feelings and unfulfilled needs. During this down time she especially needs to talk about problems and be heard and understood.

This experience is like going down into a dark well. When a women goes into her "well" she is consciously sinking into her unconscious self. She may suddenly experience a host of unexplained emotions and vague feelings. But soon after she reaches the bottom, if she feels loved and supported, she will automatically start to feel better. As suddenly as she may have crashed, she will automatically rise up and again radiate love in her relationships.

• WHEN THE WAVE CRASHES •

A man assumes that her sudden change of mood is based solely on his behavior. When she is happy he takes credit, but when she is unhappy he also feels responsible. He may feel extremely frustrated because he doesn't know how to make things better. One minute she seems happy, and so he believes he is doing a good job, and then the next minute she is unhappy. He is shocked because he thought he was doing so well.

• DON'T TRY TO FIX IT •

The last thing a woman needs when she is on her way down is someone telling her why she shouldn't be down. What she needs is someone to be with her as she goes down, to listen to her while she shares her feelings, and to empathize with what she is going through. Even if a man can't fully understand, each time he can get better at supporting her by offering his love, patience, and understanding.

A woman going into the well is not a man's fault. By being supportive, he cannot prevent it from happening, but he can help her through these difficult times.

A woman has within herself the ability to spontaneously rise up after she has hit bottom. A man does not have to fix her. She is not broken but just needs his love, patience, and understanding.

A man's love and support cannot resolve a woman's issues. His love, however, can make it safe for her to go deeper into her well. It is naive to expect a woman to be perfectly loving all the time. He can expect the issues to come up again and again. Each time, he can get better at supporting her.

THREE WAYS TO SUPPORT HER WHEN YOU NEED TO PULL AWAY

1. Accept your limitations

Accept that you need to pull away and have nothing to give. No matter how loving you want to be, you cannot listen attentively. Don't try to listen when you can't.

2. Understand her pain

She needs more than you can give at this moment. Her pain is valid. Don't make her feel she's wrong for needing more or for being hurt. It hurts to be abandoned when she needs your love.

You are not wrong for needing space,
and she is not wrong for wanting to be close.

3. Avoid arguing, give reassurance

By understanding her hurt, you won't make her feel she's wrong for being in pain. Although you can't give the support she needs, you can avoid making it worse by arguing. Reassure her that you will be back, and then you will be able to give her the support she deserves.

A woman's tendency to give too much relaxes as she remembers that she is worthy of love. She doesn't have to earn it. She can relax, give less, and receive more.

She deserves it.

If a woman doesn't feel supported when she's unhappy, then she can never truly be happy. To be genuinely happy requires dipping down into the well to release, heal, and purify the emotions. This is a natural and healthy process.

By understanding how women are like waves, men can learn how to support their partners and give them the love they deserve.

CHAPTER 7

Women are motivated and empowered
when they feel cherished.

Twenty-five Ways to Score Big on Venus

1. Surprise her with flowers.

2. Resist the temptation to solve her problems.

3. When you are going to be late, call her.

4. Don't channel surf when she's watching TV with you.

5. Take short romantic getaways.

6. Wash her car.

7. Get in bed at the same time.

8. Pay more attention to her than others in public.

9. Tell her how much you missed her when you were away.

10. Treat her the way you did when you first met.

11. Never forget her birthday.

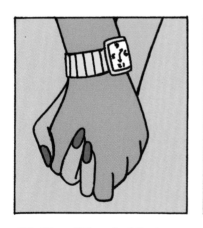

12. When holding hands, don't let your hand go limp.

13. Compliment her new look.

14. When seeing her, give her a hug before doing anything else.

15. Plan a date several days in advance.

16. Offer to help her when she's tired.

17. Practice listening and ask questions.

18. Suggest a new restaurant.

19. Open the door for her.

20. Take her side when she's upset with someone.

21. Whenever you need to "pull away," let her know that you will be back.

22. Ask her how she is feeling.

23. When listening, make eye contact.

24. Bring her presents like a small box of candy or perfume.

25. Give her a kiss and say good-bye when you leave.

CHAPTER 8

Men are motivated and empowered
when they feel needed.

Twenty-five Ways to Score Big on Mars

1. Do not give directions or unsolicited advice.

2. Be happy to see him.

3. Whenever possible, let him know, "That makes sense" or "You are right."

4. Marvel at his wit.

5. Do not reject him.

6. If he disappoints you, don't punish him.

7. Ask for support without being demanding.

8. Enjoy and admire his car.

9. Slow down when you get to the door so he can open it, and then say "thank you."

10. Really enjoy having sex with him.

11. Practice accepting imperfection.

12. Instead of fighting, take a time-out to think things over.

13. Appreciate him.

14. Admire his strength and talent.

15. When he makes a mistake don't say "I told you so."

16. If he forgets his keys, don't roll your eyes.

17. Ask his opinion.

18. When he goes into his cave, don't make him feel guilty.

19. When he comes out of his cave, be happy to see him.

20. If he says "no" to something you've asked him to do, trust that he would do it if he could.

21. Laugh at his jokes.

22. Apologize when you are wrong.

23. Be tactful when expressing your dislike about a restaurant he chose.

24. When he gets lost, see the good in the situation.

25. Always remember to kiss him good-bye.

CHAPTER 9

*Just as communication
is the most important element
in a relationship, arguments can be
the most destructive element.*

Arguments Can Hurt

One of the most difficult challenges in our loving relationships is handling differences and disagreements. Often, when couples disagree, their discussions can turn into arguments and then, without much warning, into battles. Suddenly they stop talking in a loving manner and automatically begin hurting each other: blaming, complaining, accusing, demanding, resenting, and doubting. There will always be disagreements, but we can learn a positive way to resolve them.

*Men rarely say "I'm sorry," because on Mars
it means you have done something wrong.*

Women, however, say "I'm sorry" as a way to say "I care about what you are feeling." It doesn't mean they are apologizing for doing something wrong. Men who rarely say "I am sorry" can create wonders by learning to use this aspect of the Venusian language. The easiest way to derail an argument is to say "I'm sorry."

Without understanding how men and women are different, it is very easy to get into arguments that hurt not only our partners but also ourselves. The secret to avoiding arguments is loving and respectful communication.

The differences and disagreements don't hurt as much as the ways in which we communicate them. Ideally, an argument does not have to be hurtful; instead, it can simply be an engaging conversation that expresses our differences and disagreements.

There are four stances that individuals take to avoid getting hurt in arguments. Each of these stances offers a short-term gain, but in the long run they are all counterproductive.

1. FIGHT

This stance definitely comes from Mars. When a conversation becomes unloving, many Martians move into an offensive stance. Their motto is "the best defense is a strong offense."

AVOIDING HURT

They strike out by blaming, judging, criticizing, and making their partner look wrong. When their partner backs down, they assume they have won, but in truth they have lost.

Intimidation always weakens trust in a relationship.

2. FLIGHT

This stance also comes from Mars. To avoid confrontation, Martians may retire into their caves and never come out. This is like a cold war. They refuse to talk and nothing gets resolved. These Martians don't like confrontation and would rather lie low and avoid talking about any topics that may cause an argument

3. FAKE

This stance comes from Venus. To avoid being hurt in a confrontation, many Venusians pretend that there is no problem. She puts a smile on her face and appears to be very agreeable and happy with everything. Over time, however, these women become increasingly resentful. This resentment blocks the natural expression of love.

4. FOLD

This stance also comes from Venus. Rather than argue, the Venusian gives in. She will take the blame and assume responsibility for whatever is upsetting her partner. In the short run she seems to be supportive, but she ends up losing herself.

In each of the above four stances our intention is to protect ourselves from being hurt. Unfortunately, it does not work. What works is to identify arguments and stop. Take a time-out to cool off, and then come back and talk again. Practice communicating with increased understanding and respect for the opposite sex, and you will gradually learn to avoid arguments and fights.

Reasons Venusians Argue

- "I don't like it when he minimizes the importance of my feelings."

- "I don't like it when he forgets to do the things I ask, and then I sound like a nag."

- "I don't like it when he raises his voice or starts making lists of why he is right."

- "I don't like it when he doesn't respond to my questions or comments."

- "I don't like it when he explains why I shouldn't be hurt, worried, or angry."

Reasons Martians Argue

- "I don't like it when she gets upset over the smallest things I do or don't do."

- "I don't like it when she starts telling me how I should do things."

- "I don't like it when she blames me for her unhappiness."

- "I don't like it when she worries about everything that could go wrong."

- "I don't like it when she expects me to read her mind."

Men are most prone to argue

when they have made a mistake

or upset the woman they love.

Women unknowingly start arguments

by not being direct when they

share their feelings.

CHAPTER 10

The secret of empowering a man is never try to change him or improve him.

How to Give Up Trying to Change a Man

A man needs to be accepted regardless of his imperfections. To accept a person's imperfections is not easy, especially when we see how he could become better. It does, however, become easier when we understand that the best way to help him grow is to let go of trying to change him in any way.

SIX TIPS HOW TO GIVE UP

Not Recommended

Recommended

1. Don't ask too many questions when he is upset.

Ignore that he is upset unless he wants to talk to you about it. Show some initial concern, but not too much, as an invitation to talk.

TRYING TO CHANGE A MAN

Not Recommended

Well! If you want my opinion,
I say ask for that raise, and while you're
at it, ask for an extra week of vacation.

Recommended

I'm sure
you'll do
what's best.

2. Wait until he asks for your advice.

Practice patience, and trust that he will learn on his own
what he needs to learn. When you offer unsolicited advice,
he may feel mistrusted, controlled, or rejected.

3. Practice accepting imperfection.

Make his feelings more important than perfection. Try not to lecture or correct him.

Not Recommended

Recommended

4. Don't make sacrifices.

If you make sacrifices hoping he will do the same for you, then he will feel pressured to change. Practice doing things for yourself and do not depend on him to make you happy.

When negative feelings

are suppressed, positive feelings

become suppressed as well,

and love dies. Take time

to share your feelings

Phew! I'm exhausted. So much to do, so little time. What's a girl to do?

Recommended

I've had an awful day. It would help to talk about it. All you have to do is listen.

5. You can share negative feelings without trying to change him.

When sharing feelings, let him know that you are not trying to tell him what to do, but that you want him to take your feelings into consideration. When he feels accepted it is easier for him to listen.

Not Recommended

Recommended

6. Practice forgiveness.

Forgive his mistakes. He may resist admitting to mistakes to avoid rejection. Practice showing him that he doesn't have to be perfect to receive your love.

Just as men want to explain why women shouldn't be upset, women want to explain why men shouldn't behave the way they do. Just as men mistakenly want to "fix" women, women mistakenly try to "improve" men.

Men see the world through Martian eyes. Their motto is "Don't fix it if it isn't broken." When a woman attempts to change a man, he receives the message that she thinks he is broken. This makes him very defensive. He doesn't feel loved and accepted.

The best way to help a man grow is to let go of trying to change him in any way.

CHAPTER 11

If a woman is not asking for support,
a man assumes he is giving enough.

How to Ask for Support and Get It

Many women make the mistake of thinking they don't have to ask for support. Because they intuitively feel the needs of others and give whatever they can, they mistakenly expect men to do the same. Men are not instinctively motivated to offer their support; they need to be asked.

STEP 1.

Ask for What You Are Already Getting

- Become aware of and acknowledge what your partner is already doing for you. Especially the little things, like carrying boxes, fixing things, making reservations, and other chores.

- Begin asking him to do the things you know he's willing to do. When he does those things, appreciate him.

- Temporarily give up expecting him to offer unsolicited support.

- In the beginning, do not ask for more than what he is used to giving. Practice the five tips for asking.

Five Asking Tips

1. Timing is crucial.

Be careful not to ask him to do something that he is obviously just planning to do. For example, if he is about to empty the trash, don't say "Could you empty the trash?"

2. Use a nondemanding attitude.

A request is not a demand. If you have a resentful or demanding attitude, no matter how carefully you choose your words, he will feel unappreciated and probably say no.

3. Be brief.

Avoid giving him a list of reasons why he should help you. Long explanations validating your request make him feel as though you don't trust him to support you.

When asking for support, assume that he doesn't have to be convinced.

 **Be direct.**

Women often think they are asking for support when they are not. A woman may present the problem but not directly ask for his support. She expects him to offer his support.

Not Recommended	*Recommended*
"The kids need to be picked up and I can't do it."	"Would you pick up the kids?"
"The mail hasn't been brought in."	"Would you bring in the mail?"
"We haven't gone out in weeks."	"Let's do something fun. Would you plan a date?"

Men always respond best to direct requests
as opposed to implied requests.

5. Use correct wording.

By using correct wording, a man will be more motivated to provide what a woman wants.

One of the most common mistakes in asking for support is the use of "could" and "can" in place of "would" and "will." "Could you empty the trash?" is merely a question gathering information. "Would you empty the trash?" is a request.

Use the "w" words. The "c" words sound too untrusting, indirect, weak, and manipulative.

Practice Asking for More
(EVEN WHEN YOU KNOW HE MAY SAY NO)

Before attempting to ask a man for more, make sure he feels appreciated for what he is already giving. When a man feels appreciated for what he is giving, then it's time to ask for more in small increments.

In step 2, your objective is to ask for more while also giving the message he can say no and still receive your love and support.

Pick situations where you would appreciate his support but rarely ask for it. Use this approach only for situations that are really OK if he says no.

If You Want to Get, You Have to Ask

He is very busy with an important project. You don't want to distract him because you sense how focused he is, but you also want to talk with him. Normally, you would not ask for some time, but you are practicing asking for more.

Men are much more willing to say yes
if they have the freedom to say no.

STEP 3.

Practice Assertive Asking

Once you have practiced step 2 and can graciously accept a no, you are ready for step 3. In this step you assert your full power to get what you want. You ask for his support, and if he starts making excuses, you don't say "OK," as in step 2. Instead, practice making it OK that he resists, but continue waiting for him to say yes.

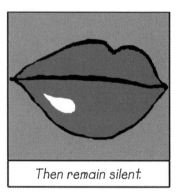

One of the key elements

of assertive asking is to remain silent

after you have asked for support.

If you break the silence,

you lose your power.

On Venus, the motto is "Love is never having to ask!"

Because this is her reference point, she assumes that if her partner loves her, he will offer his support and she won't have to ask. She may even purposefully not ask as a test to see if he really loves her. To pass the test, she requires that he anticipate her needs and offer his unsolicited support!

This approach to relationships with men doesn't work. Men are from Mars, and on Mars, if you want support, you simply have to ask for it.

By learning the art of asking for support, your relationships will gradually become greatly enriched. As you are able to receive more of the love and support you need, your partner will also naturally be happy. Men are happiest when they feel they have succeeded in fulfilling the people they care about.

By learning to ask correctly for support, you not only help your man feel more loved, but you also ensure that you'll get the love you need and deserve.

CHAPTER 12

Writing down your feelings
is an essential tool.

The Feeling Letter

When we are upset, frustrated, or angry, it is difficult to communicate lovingly. At such times, talking turns to fighting. These are the times when talking does not work.

Fortunately, there is another alternative. Instead of verbally sharing your feelings with your partner, write him or her a letter. Writing letters allows you to listen to your own feelings without worrying about hurting your partner. By freely expressing and listening to your feelings, you automatically become more centered and loving. Then there is no need to share your letter. Once you are feeling warm and friendly, you can focus on finding a solution without dwelling on the problem.

Writing the feeling letter

1. Give yourself about twenty minutes.

2. Find a quiet spot and address the letter to your partner. Pretend that he or she is listening to you with love and understanding. You will not give your partner this letter. It is for your benefit only.

3. Start with anger, then sadness, then fear, then regret. Write a few sentences expressing each of these four levels of emotion.

After each section, pause and notice the next feeling coming up. Write about that feeling. The most releasing expressions are "I am angry," "I am sad," "I am afraid," and "I am sorry."

Our emotions are like an iceberg:
We generally are aware of only a small fraction;
the rest remains submerged.

4. By first exploring your negative emotions, automatically your positive feelings will begin to emerge. Take a few minutes to think about and express what you want, need, or wish, and then move on to express positive feelings of love, appreciation, forgiveness, and trust.

5. Sign your name at the end. Express the response you would like to hear from your partner.

Sample Feeling Letter About Arguing

Dear Vanessa,

Anger: *I am angry that you get so emotional. I am angry that you are so sensitive. I am angry that you mistrust and reject me.*

Sadness: *I am sad that we are arguing. It hurts to lose your love. I am sad that we fought. I am sad that we disagree.*

Fear: *I am afraid of making a mistake. I am afraid you do not appreciate me. I am afraid to talk with you when you are so upset.*

Regret: *I am sorry I hurt you. I am sorry I don't agree with you. I am sorry that I make your feelings wrong. I am sorry that I judged you.*

Love: *I love you and I want to work this out. I love you. This time, when we talk, I will be more understanding.*

I love you,
Michael

P.S. The response I would like to hear is "I love you, Michael. I really appreciate what a caring and understanding man you are."

Love brings up
our unresolved feelings

Angry

Defensive

Demanding

Numb

Irritable

Critical

Healing the Past

One day we are feeling loved, and the next day we are suddenly afraid to trust love. The painful memories of being rejected begin to surface when we are faced with trusting our partner's love.

Feelings that we could not express in our past may suddenly flood our consciousness when we are safe to feel. Love thaws out our repressed feelings, and gradually these unresolved feelings begin to surface into our relationship.

It is as though your unresolved feelings wait until you are feeling loved, and then they come up to be healed.

The 90/10 Principle

By understanding how unresolved
past feelings periodically surface,
we can understand why we become
so easily hurt by our partners.
When we are upset, about 90
percent of the upset is related
to our past and has nothing to do
with what we think is upsetting us.
Generally, only about 10 percent
of our upset is appropriate to
the present experience.

· A HEALING LETTER ·

Understanding how your past affects your present reactions helps you heal your feelings. If your partner has upset you in some way, write them a Healing Letter, and while you are writing, ask yourself how this relates to your past. As you write, you may find memories coming up to reveal unresolved feelings from your past. At this point, continue writing, but as if you are in the past.

Take a few minutes to explore and heal your past using the Feeling Letter format (page 113).

By getting to the root cause of your upset, you are then free to appreciate and trust your partner in present time.

CHAPTER 13

Love is seasonal.

The Seasons of Love

A relationship is like a garden. If it is to thrive it must be watered regularly. Special care must be given, taking into account the seasons as well as any unpredictable weather. New seeds must be sown and weeds must be pulled. Similarly, to keep the magic of love alive we must understand its seasons and nurture love's special needs.

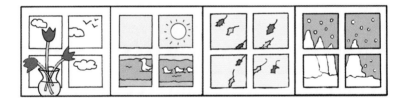

The Springtime of Love

Falling in love is like springtime. We feel as though we will be happy forever. It is a time of innocence. Love seems eternal. Our partner seems to be the perfect fit. We effortlessly dance together in harmony and rejoice in our good fortune.

The Summer of Love

Throughout the summer of our love we realize our partner is not as perfect as we thought, and we have to work on our relationship. Frustration and disappointment arise; weeds need to be uprooted and plants need extra watering under the hot sun.

It is no longer easy to give love and get the love we need. Couples blame their partners and give up. They do not realize that love is not always easy; sometimes it requires hard work under a hot sun. In the summer season of love, we need to nurture our partner's needs as well as ask for and get the love we need. It doesn't happen automatically.

The Autumn of Love

As a result of tending the garden during the summer, we get to harvest the results of our hard work. Fall has come. It is a golden time—rich and fulfilling. We experience a more mature love that accepts and understands our partner's imperfections as well as our own. It is a time of thanksgiving and sharing. Having worked hard during the summer, we can relax and enjoy the love we have created.

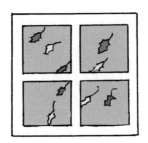

The Winter of Love

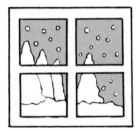

Then the weather changes again, and winter comes. During the cold, barren months of winter, all of nature pulls back within itself. It is a time of rest, reflection, and renewal. It is a time of solitary growth when we need to look more to ourselves than to our partners for love and fulfillment. It is a time of healing. This is the time when men hibernate in their caves and women sink to the bottom of their wells.

After loving and healing ourselves through the dark winter of love, then spring inevitably returns. Once again we are blessed with the feelings of hope, love, and an abundance of possibilities. Based on the inner healing and soul-searching of our winter journey, we are now able to open our hearts and feel the springtime of love.

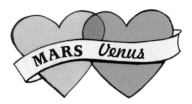

Next time you are frustrated with the
opposite sex, remember: Men are from Mars
and women are from Venus.

Even if you don't remember anything
else from this book, remembering that we
are supposed to be different will help
you to be more loving.

You have a lot to look forward to.
May you continue to grow in love and light.
Thank you for letting me make
a difference in your life.

SPECIAL OFFER FOR YOU

Call 1-888-627-7836 for details on receiving
a free 10-minute coaching session.

Now you have the ability to talk with a MARS VENUS
expert when an issue comes up.
We all understand the power of information.
The more we know, the better we can deal with a situation.
No matter how successful we are, sometimes we all need to
talk about our problems to understand them better.

We have analyzed your most frequently asked questions
about relationships and have developed a coaching program
that not only provides information about the cause of
and solution to your problem, but also provides
a coach to guide you through your situation.

Call today for information about this service and you'll
receive a free 10-minute coaching session.

Your special pin number entitles you to one free 10-minute coaching session.

PIN = 527235

This pin number should only be used once.

Also, one caller per month will randomly be selected to speak to
John Gray personally for a free 20-minute session.

If you like what you have read, and you want more for your company, organization, or yourself, consider:

MARS VENUS IN THE WORKPLACE SEMINARS

Thousands of individuals and companies around the world have already benefited from John Gray's workplace seminars. We invite you to share an inspiring presentation or workshop with your company. MARS VENUS IN THE WORKPLACE seminars are designed to enhance gender communication in the workplace at all levels. Presentations are made by John Gray or one of his many trainers. Each seminar can easily be tailored to the unique needs of your company or organization. Please call our representatives toll-free at 1-888-MARSVENUS (1-888-627-7836) or visit John Gray's website at www.marsvenus.com for booking information.

ATTENDING A MARS VENUS WORKSHOP

The MARS VENUS INSTITUTE offers workshops that bring information to local communities and organizations around the world and trains those interested in presenting these workshops. MARS VENUS workshops focus on different topics, including improving communication, understanding differences, dating, starting over, parenting, and achieving personal success. These fun and insightful workshops feature favorite video segments from live seminars by John Gray, along with workbooks and exercises for participants to apply the information. A current schedule of workshops available throughout the world can be found on the website. To facilitate a workshop for your school, church, organization, or community, please call 1-888-MARSVENUS (1-888-627-7836). Becoming a facilitator is easy. You can be trained to present these workshops over the internet or through correspondence.

MARS VENUS COUNSELING CENTERS

In response to the thousands of requests we have received for licensed professionals who use the MARS VENUS principles in their practices, John Gray has provided a training program for licensed professionals to provide the MARS VENUS approach to their clients. Participants in this program have completed a rigorous study of John's work and have demonstrated a commitment to his valuable concepts. If you are interested in a referral to a counselor in your area or you seek information to be trained as a MARS VENUS counselor or to establish a MARS VENUS counseling center, please call 1-888-MARSVENUS (1-888-627-7836).

TALK TO A MARS VENUS RELATIONSHIP COACH

Reading John Gray's books and listening to his tapes have helped millions of individuals to improve communication and get what they want in their relationships. Whether you are single or married, it is never too late or too early to understand the ways men and women are different. This valuable resource can be enriched by talking to a MARS VENUS relationship coach on the phone.

When you feel the need to talk with someone like you or of the opposite sex, who is also familiar with the MARS VENUS principals and insights, he or she is only a phone call away. By calling a MARS VENUS coach you will receive personal attention to your specific needs. In the privacy of your own home, with complete anonymity, you can freely share your concerns and questions to sort out what you feel and then decide what you want to do. You decide when and how long you want to talk. Call 1-888-MARSVENUS (1-888-627-7836) or visit www.askmarsvenus.com.

EXPLORE THE WORLD OF JOHN GRAY AT MARSVENUS.COM

At www.marsvenus.com you will find information on the following subjects:

- John Gray's free weekly newsletter
- Workshops, seminars, coaching, and counseling
- John's weekly question-and-answer column
- The MARS VENUS Dating Site
- The MARS VENUS Store
- John's Calendar
- How to become a MARS VENUS facilitator, coach or counselor
- Insight, advice, and shared experiences from all of John Gray's books and tapes, from personal relationships and parenting to achieving greater success at work

If you do not have internet access and would like the information on any of the above topics, please call toll-free 1-888-MARSVENUS (1-888-627-7836).

SHOP ONLINE AT THE MARS VENUS STORE

John's books, audio and video programs, and game are developed for all ages and stages of relationships. You can purchase all of his products easily online when you visit the store at www.marsvenus.com. Each week a different program is discounted specially for MARS VENUS online visitors.

If you don't have internet access and desire further explorations of the wonderful world of Mars and Venus, or if you wish to make an order or receive additional information, please call toll-free 1-888-MARSVENUS (1-888-627-7836).

www.marsvenus.com

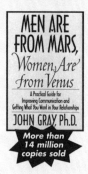

BECAUSE PERSONAL DYNAMICS
CAN MAKE THE DIFFERENCE

MARS AND VENUS IN THE WORKPLACE
*A Practical Guide for Improving
Communication and Getting Results at Work*

Hardcover 0-06-019796-X
Audio versions read by the author:
6 cassettes / 9 hours (unabridged) 0-694-52655-X
2 cassettes / 2.5 hours (abridged) 0-694-52555-3
2 compact discs / 2.5 hours (abridged) 0-694-52560-X

MAKE PARENTING A
POSITIVE EXPERIENCE

CHILDREN ARE FROM HEAVEN
*Positive Parenting Skills for Raising Cooperative,
Confident, and Compassionate Children*

Trade paperback 0-06-093099-3
Audio versions read by the author:
2 cassettes / 2.5 hours (abridged) 0-694-52136-1
2 compact discs / 2.5 hours (abridged) 0-694-52170-1
7 cassettes (unabridged) 0-694-52163-9

CHANGE YOUR LIFE!

HOW TO GET WHAT YOU WANT AND WANT WHAT YOU HAVE
A Practical and Spiritual Guide to Personal Success

Trade paperback 0-06-093215-5 • Large Print 0-06-093307-0
Audio versions read by the author:
2 compact discs / 2 hours (abridged) 0-694-52177-9
2 cassettes / 2 hours (abridged) 0-694-52179-5
6 cassettes / 9 hours (unabridged) 0-694-52178-7

PRACTICAL MIRACLES FOR MARS AND VENUS
*Nine Principles for Lasting Love, Increasing Success,
and Vibrant Health in the Twenty-first Century*

Trade paperback 0-06-093730-0 • Large Print 0-06-019950-4
Audio versions read by the author:
7 compact discs / 9 hours (unabridged) 0-694-52371-2
6 cassettes / 9 hours (unabridged) 0-694-52372-0

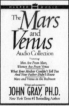
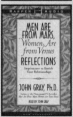

VIDEOS BY JOHN GRAY
JOHN GRAY TWO-PACK VHS VIDEOTAPE SERIES

In these five 2-pack VHS tape series, Dr. John Gray explains how differences between men and women—Martians and Venusians—can develop mutually fulfilling and loving relationships. Series includes:

MEN ARE FROM MARS, WOMEN ARE FROM VENUS
(2-Pack #1)
Tape #1: Improving Communication (60 mins.)
Tape #2: How to Motivate the Opposite Sex (56 mins.)

MARS AND VENUS IN THE BEDROOM
(2-Pack #2)
Tape #1: Great Sex (80 mins.)
Tape #2: The Secrets of Passion (47 mins.)

MARS AND VENUS TOGETHER FOREVER
Understanding the Cycles of Intimacy
(2-Pack #3)
Tape #1: Men Are Like Rubber Bands (45 mins.)
Tape #2: Women Are Like Waves (62 mins.)

MARS AND VENUS ON A DATE
(2-Pack #4)
Tape #1: Navigating the Five Stages of Dating (57 mins.)
Tape #2: The Secrets of Attraction (71 mins.)

MARS AND VENUS STARTING OVER
(2-Pack #5)
Tape #1: Finding Love Again (107 mins.)
Tape #2: The Gift of Healing (105 mins.)

For further exploration of the wonderful world of Mars and Venus,
please call or write to place an order for additional information.

John Gray Seminars
20 Sunnyside Avenue #A-130
Mill Valley, CA 94941-1564
1-888-MARSVENUS (1-888-627-7836)